Concert and Contest COLLECTION

Compiled and Edited by H. VOXMAN

T0079594

for ▶ Solo Trombone (Bass Clef)

TROMBONE with piano accompaniment

CONTENTS

RUBANK®

HAL•LEONARD® CORPORATION

7777 W. BLUEMOUND RD. P.O. BOX 13819 MILWAUKEE, WI 53213

## COLLECTIONS IN THIS SERIES:

C Flute and Piano

B♭ Clarinet and Piano

B♭ Bass Clarinet and Piano

Oboe and Piano

Bassoon and Piano

E♭ Alto Saxophone and Piano

B♭ Tenor Saxophone and Piano

B♭ Cornet, Trumpet
or Baritone and Piano
(Baritone In Bass or Treble Clef)

French Horn (In F) and Piano

Trombone (Bass Clef) and Piano

E♭ or BB♭ Bass
(Tuba - Sousaphone) and Piano

Viola and Piano

**Individually Compiled and Edited, Each Of the Collections Includes A Diversified Repertoire
The Solo Parts and Piano Accompaniments Are Published As Separate Books With A Durable Cover**

# Après un Rêve
## (After A Dream)

**Trombone**

GABRIEL FAURÉ, Op. 7, No. 1
Transcribed by H. Voxman

# Valse Sentimentale

Trombone

P. I. TSCHAIKOWSKY
Transcribed by H. Voxman

# Canzonetta

Trombone

W. A. MOZART
Adapted by H. Voxman

# Two Spanish Dances

**Trombone**

LEROY OSTRANSKY

## I

# II

# Thème de Concours

Trombone

ROBERT CLÉRISSE
Edited by H. Voxman

# Sarabande and Vivace

Trombone

G. F. HANDEL
Transcribed by H. Voxman

# Love Thoughts

Trombone

ARTHUR PRYOR
Transcribed by Clair W. Johnson

Trombone

# Morceau de Concours

**Trombone**

EDMOND MISSA
Edited by H. Voxman

*Eb in + 6th position,
lip trill to F.

# Crépuscule
## (Twilight)

Trombone

GABRIEL PARÈS
Edited by H. Voxman

# Concerto Miniature

Trombone

LEROY OSTRANSKY

# Prelude and Fanfaronade

Trombone

PAUL KOEPKE

# Solo de Concert

Trombone

Th. DUBOIS
Edited by H. Voxman

Trombone

# Concerto in F Minor

Trombone

ÉMILE LAUGA
Edited by H. Voxman

# Allegro Vivace
## from Concerto

Trombone

Edited by H. Voxman

N. RIMSKY - KORSAKOFF
Arr. by N. Fedossejew

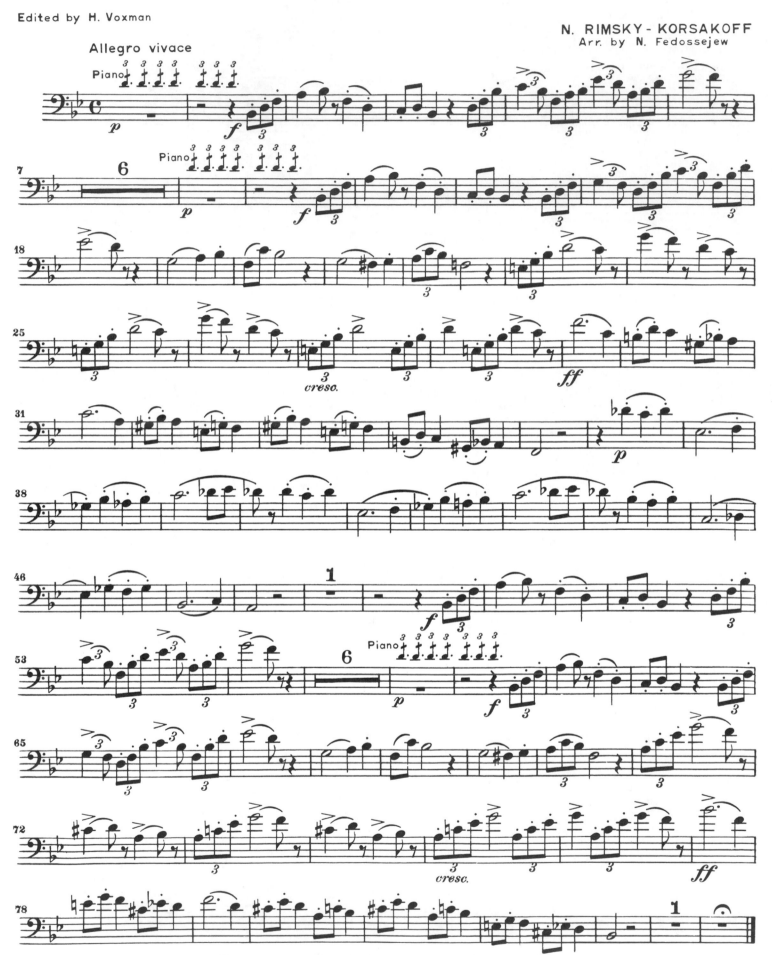